D1594722

THE ADA POEMS

Cynthia Zarin

THE ADA POEMS

ALFRED A. KNOPF · NEW YORK · 2010

This Is a Borzoi Book
Published by Alfred A. Knopf

Copyright © 2010 by Cynthia Zarin

All rights reserved. Published in the United States by Alfred A. Knopf,
a division of Random House, Inc., New York, and in Canada by
Random House of Canada, Limited, Toronto.

www.aaknopf.com

Knopf, Borzoi Books, and the colophon are registered trademarks of
Random House, Inc.

Library of Congress Cataloging-in-Publication Data
Zarin, Cynthia.
    The Ada poems / by Cynthia Zarin.——1st ed.
        p. cm.
ISBN 978-0-307-27247-8
1. Nabokov, Vladimir Vladimirovich, 1899–1977. Ada——Poetry. I. Title.
PS3576.A69A65 2010
811'.54——dc22   2010002608

Manufactured in the United States of America
First Edition

"All right. What was the other game?"

"The other game (in a singsong voice) might seem a little more complicated. To play it properly one had to wait for P.M. to provide longer shadows. The player—"

"Stop saying 'the player.' It is either you or me."

—VLADIMIR NABOKOV, *Ada, or Ardor: A Family Chronicle*

Eines ist, die Geliebte zu singen. Ein anderes, wehe,
jenen verborgenen schuldigen Fluß-Gott des Bluts.

—RAINER MARIA RILKE, *Duino Elegies*

Nec mortem effugere quisquam nec amorem potest.

—SYRUS, *Maxims*

CONTENTS

THE ADA POEMS

BIRCH

Bone-spur, stirrup of veins—white colt
a tree, sapling bone again, worn to a splinter,
    a steeple, the birch aground

in its ravine of leaves. Abide with me, arrive
at its skinned branches, its arms pulled
      from the sapling, your wrist taut,

each ganglion a gash in the tree's rent
trunk, a child's hackwork, *love plus love,*
      my palms in your fist, that

trio a trident splitting the birch, its bark
papyrus, its scars calligraphy,
      a ghost story written on

winding sheets, the trunk bowing, *dead is*
my father, the birch reading the news
      of the day aloud as if we hadn't

heard it, the root moss lit gas,
like the veins on your ink-stained hand—
      the birch all elbows, taking us in.

AESOP

" 'Our black rainbow,' Ada termed it, '. . . inside a grille of rain.' "

Cold on each leaf, cut glass, cold where you are—
at dawn my palms cross-hatched by tiny cuts
as if sharp-beaked birds had tried to eat but
finding nothing pecked instead. What knock-kneed
gentled monkey salves and holds the cat's
burnt paw? Nothing makes this right but that it
is—wild for twenty years, in Ektachrome,
you've buttoned your old jacket wrong; the cast
die said you can't redo it, or this, or
graze from my hand. Chastened, what can we do
but mutter, talk, and read? Dear heart, the years
caught up with us. Like tortoises, they've passed
the too-sure hare, and racing, gone ahead—
daring us—posthumous—to live on air.

REGIME

Two days of no word—or three—I imagine
Pound's letter, the cold blue plums—Imogene
cast out; her card marked: death by fen, by fire.
Mute, woe woos both beggar-maid and chooser
but my woe is marriage. We balk and shy.
Your voice is gravel, chalk, convoking star.
I wake to dream. You who are not here—not
here. How far would I come to meet you?
The road is thick with snow, the river black ice—
in your father's clothes you turn to smoke, then
skywriting. This fall, driving north, and north—
the shaken world awash, myrmidon, swot
ambergris—the fierce trees with their platelet
streams, each leaf a handprint, corporeal.

FIRST DREAMSCAPE

No one but lovers and children tell their dreams:
not fish, nearer fowl, where does that leave me—
bantam in the barnyard, pecking for mash.
Bleak lovebirds, our nests are spangled with remorse
and love; for us the order out of kilter:
what we love, we burn. In the dream, Devon,
Kentisbeare, winter, but the lawns still
green, the stone church black with wet against
the brackish sky, the mourners quickly off
in twos and threes—abashed at talking yet
they still went on. I was the dreamer—dead,
I had to choose. The scene tilted. The emerald
air was now the scuffed mill's cuckoo cloud.
Twice shy. I'd never left except with you.

CHRISTMAS I

"She was on bad terms with memory."

No longer able to think or write or breathe—
New York a cynosure of drink and guilt,
the sweetheart roses tilt their faces
to the piano's black sateen bat wing.
Before the shoe is thrown and King Rat falls
there's Queen Victoria in bombazine
a bleary tear sheet bunched to feed the flames.
I sit on the stairs and stare. The snapdragons
open their pale throats to sneeze—chrysanthemum
smell of burning hair. Below, our old tortoise
paces the scorched carpet. On his armoured back
a sparkler shooting red and green. One letter
less, *amour* is his world. Whose name is Mother?
I hardly know my hand that struck the match.

CHRISTMAS (NIGHT) II

The tattered damask splits and blurs like script,
rosettes of warp and woof too small to read—
but some letters, you'd say, are better left
unread, or burned. When we went to visit
the Queen Mother, Mama wouldn't let us stay
for fear the candles would ignite the tree—
On the mantel, the Nutcracker girl curtsies
but cannot, will not bow—her "Aztec" dress
a fin de siècle fantasy. *When I think*
—don't. Shadow-hare, your name writes itself.
"He wants a wife who—" Dumb-show fool,
I mime death by sword, death by water.
After all this time? Mnemosyne asks,
then shrugs, her sequined green gaze cloaked, a hiss.

FOG IN HOLYOKE

" 'Oh, look at those sea gulls playing chicken.' "

Four days after Christmas, fog skims the river—
thin skin a skein of yarn after yarn, knotted
with sleet, moth grey. Headlights on. Albertine
and Lara, ghostly aunts playing cards, float
by the cataract eye of the skating rink;
then, wraiths draped in gauze, through the paper mill
wall. "Twenty years ago," you said, "who knew?
You were on track and I was foundering."
Derelict, my heart, time-fish hooked in fog.
A pause. Tears in my mouth like spawn, like stars,
those stars your hands, hand over hand, my kneecaps
bright, drawn up, the brick wall beyond the broken
sash copper in the streetlight. I never thought
you couldn't take care of an animal.

SECOND DREAMSCAPE
(NEW YEAR'S NIGHT)

The road we walked in winter was a figure eight.
In the cabin, Möbius's flypaper strip dangled
from the ceiling, its amber isinglass. Pines
pressed in, fish bones, quill scales dead upright
—a feather headdress, finished here and there
with diamond filigree—and the ceiling was the sky,
a snow globe where it kept snowing
on the covered bridge, and the barn,
and the moon rose like a quarter but shone
only if you could guess—*heads or tails*—
but even if the man in the moon wouldn't speak
and turned his back and put on his hat
light shone anyway on his white hair
and we walked and walked until the hemisphere
split like an orange, and we were back
inside. It was very late. The strip
had caught more flies than we could count
and a spider too, a miniature miracle,
all legs and eyes, and the green feathers
were still dipped in snow.

NEW MEXICO/SANGRE DE CRISTO MOUNTAINS/EPIPHANY

" . . . a tiny theater that specialized in Painted Westerns."

The fir trees Russian in their tulle of snow,
their children ravens in hemstitched chemises
allowed up late to see the Kings.
At Jemez Pueblo, boys at once too young,
too old, their ladder Jacob's own beneath
the cow-faced clouds, pretend to fly and fall,
then catch themselves, until the blue-faced
buffalos—their uncles—make them stop
and stare. I never thought you couldn't take
care of—*fill in the blanks.* Why can't I want
anything I want? Drumbeats. Caws. And though
we asked and asked, no one could tell us where
the Madonna was, our breath resin, the mist
a houri hired by the hour to ogle the moon.

LETTER

Older, slyer. Silence spent, for days we've
sped and shied. My country stands and falls
with and without you—last night cop cars,
sharks outside the house; scenting fear, they have
no choice but to school and whir. Nothing
tears me from blood sport, ganglia singing—
sand under my spine and you intent, a boy
hearing his own name as birdsong, counting
my pulse, a tern darting. Daedalus, whose
spokes set the sea afire—-nothing we kept
did anything but burn, each hair singed by
the cigarette's acrid kiss. Needle bent,
my rattletrap compass shuns the North Star's pull;
your wet hand stung by the eel's charged swerve.

LETTER TWO

" 'Destroy and forget,' said Ada."

Lost ring, lost shoe, lost fortune, fortune found—
what blessing is a burden when its head is turned?
The Jack of Spades become the Suicide King,
loss by way of love and lose. Bee sting.
The mind swells, ricochets until every card
has your face. The black cat's languor, snarled
as yarn, turns into morning's yawning hall
of mirrors. Do you remember our walks
along the Hudson, the trashed seventies washing up,
girding the houseboats with gilt flotsam?
Fervent croupier, all hands and eyes, your
mascara an inked gate that would slam down—
blame is Gilead's crop, he jokes for food.
I'd trade every moment for any moment.

ANODYNE

For years I tried to write
about bloody Jack and his mad Queen,
their tallow figures pierced by swords,
mirror emblem of a dogged dream.

But my pen was a sparrow
that could or would not light
beneath the Snow Queen's shadow.
Then time pulled the slipknot tight.

Behind the skit's black fire screen
where nothing ever is put right,
everything is as it seems—
stunned beauty, where my heart is moored,

the moon, that fretted boat let go.

MONDAY RHYME (KHARTOUM)

"Oh, write me, one tiny note . . . ?"

I love you in the desert
I love you by the shore
My love for you is a windward ship
How could I ask for more?

It flies across the continents
Bold frigate, carpet, centaur
Brash rainbow studded with sylvan bells—
Why would I ask for more?

Love, the years are legion
The past was white and noir
You were on the snow-lashed steppes—
I fished without a lure.

Now the moon has rattled
The starry dipper poured—
If years mean far from where you are
I stop at any more.

GREEK POEM

You came out of winter
   approaching.
Death and more death
  and my heart was
cold to you.

You said:
  talk to me.
I was
  a stone
thrown in the river.

We spoke. We were
 as children, speaking.
Then not—
   my head bent back.

Not quiet.

      o

—quick fish—scales—lapis—
 child practicing scales—

      o

You asked me to come
    and I did.

  Where were you?
you asked, if I slept.

And then you took
　　out your stock

of silence, those thick
　　dry goods.

You are a managing director
　　of silence.

I should have
known
　　that silence

anywhere.

And I should not
　　have listened to you
at the river.

But I was happy
　　to hear your
voice again—

the sound
　　of my heart beating.

It is my own fault
　　that I listened

　　to you, to that
　　　lyre in the reeds.

AUBADE AGAINST GRIEF

Chaste sun who would not light your face
pale as the fates
    who vanished

when we turned aside; recluse
whom grace
      returned and by returning banished

all thought but: Love, late
sleeper in the early hours, flesh of my bone,
    centaur: Excuse

my faults—tardiness, obtuse
remit of my own
    heart, unruly haste

to keep my mouth on yours, to wipe the slate
clean, to atone—
    what could I want but to wait

for that light to touch your face,
chaste as Eros in the first wished-
    on rush of wings?

SPRING THAW

"... that tattered chapbook ..."

My left hand has never known my right.
The tinderbox it keeps to strike

the matchstick house my right hand built
by drawing and redrawing lines

like someone who can't love or learn
or read the reeling smoke's too-likely scrawl.

I wrote that, too, above the house I drew.
Can't, or won't. My heart's not right.

My right hand saves what my left burns
as if what's left—that black cloud, those few

reticulate, neglected trees—could be kept
where everything but what you want is free.

To draw a circus tent, and not a house!
As if I could—velvet swags, a white

cat whose kittens are bows on a kite
string, a solitary dog, hermaphrodite

who loves himself both day and night.
(His? her? pinhole-parasol lets teardrops fall.)

Let's stop—*no*—and name him Aphrodite.
I could go on and on, being free—

freehand, that is. But I wish I'd known—
earlier, how it would feel, what might

go wrong, what hurt, what didn't, after all.
Or if the two-stroke charcoal roof could bear

a row of exponential birds in azure air.

APRIL
(ABOARD THE *HALF MOON*)

The minutes rickshaws strung with fairy lights—
better just to read and gaze, the river slips,
amethyst to tourmaline, lapping—
>   *interrupt, interrupt, rip up, rip up——:*
>   late, *I couldn't wake to catch a plane.*
The clock ticked fourteen over Westbourne Grove—
     the paintbrush irises were second hands.
In the junkshop, King Edward's valet's sofa,
tattered mauve, held court beneath a vale
of crystal tears. Do you remember the wolf
who baited shadow rabbits on the wall
of our West End Avenue fourth-story dive?
He was too dear and ragged to leave home.

This in magic marker on a paper plate.

POEM FOR A PRINTING PRESS

"... dubious words in a number of lexicons [...]"

A is for angel
B is for bone
C is a carillon
D is a doe
E isn't easy
F wants to fly
G is for gee whiz
H says hiss
I is for impulse
J is for jewel
K is a kitty hawk
L is for lose
M sends a message
N says no
P is the piper
Q calls it quits
R is for red
S is the snake
T is for troubles
U stays up late
V is for vanquish
W asks why
X is an answer
Y is for yes
Z is for zed

But wait—
O—*oh*—rolled away.

ELECTRIC LIGHT

"('True, my lovely and larveless.')"

The dragonfly whirs and whirs and will not stop
replaying its ceaseless hum over the tightly pulled rungs
of wire at the topmost end of the scale.
Fire runs along the wires as if someone had wrapped
the sound in rags and lit a match. St. George
in his emerald livery, his tiny jeweled sword drawn, has no time
   for this domestic crisis, more darning needle
than dragon, who with ragged black stitches tries
to sew up the seam while busily sawing the air
    with its tarnished wings
but the tear is there.
Through it I see the blue scribbled-on sky over the sea
where a quiver of dragonflies draws frantic lines
over the high weed-choked rocky dunes.
It wasn't this summer, I don't think so, but the summer before
   last.
Hot, glassine—no one
knew why they had come nor why were there so many of
   them—obviously speaking
to each other in a language made up of static
fueled by the sun, the sound of steel wool
on a washboard, filling the space between earth
and air by writing over and over it,
          as my hand does here
—if only one could swallow the sword and be done with it—
leaving no place, under the din of the white-hot filament
of the reading light, free of your name.

THIRD DREAMSCAPE

"There are people who can fold a road map."

I *NEW AMSTERDAM–COLRAIN*

The rain all night made rivulets in the garden
between the flagstones and the ferns, which were
just starting to unfold their fan fronds underneath
the sky's turned-down indigo cup. The rain broke up
the earth into islands and promontories flecked
here and there with green—moss, I think, though it's
too early and too cold. Rain raced down the window,
a no-legged race played out to nothing.
The tears behind my lids are more fire than water.
What does the fire say? Black heart, white ash.
Outside, the mockingbird hoots
but does not answer. Hecuba, barking.
Your sure hand in the dog's fur. Too early. You're sleeping too.
It's snowing where you are. The dark-rimmed dog's eye
is the sun behind a raindrop, an eclipse, a peeled rind.

II *ORVIETO*

It wasn't Ravenna, it was—I had to look it up
in the bookcase under the stairs, in the blue guidebook—
I was looking for a place to buy a shoelace, apparently,
in 1980. There it is, carefully written out, *merletti.*
The corner turned down, the penciled circle smeared
to a rain cloud: how strange rereading doesn't wear
print off the page.

                    Could it be there still, the shop
with its row of priests' shoes, tongues barely
bound by the gnarled laces?
A pair of gold evening slippers was strung up in the window
next to a dried palm cross. (One tongue is Hecuba's,
thumping her tail in the dream.)
And the slippers, who lost them, or bought them?
Hazelnut, chocolate, strawberry, tiramisu—at the *gelateria*
the ices were set in a compass wheel
under the counter, a frozen scoop marking every direction on
    earth,
the last, blood orange, set in a hollowed-out rind threaded with
    white capillaries,
                    a pink emergency,
and in the piazza, the black-and-white cathedral, built
to commemorate the miracle at Bolzano, six
kilometers away, when blood dripped from an altar cloth
"and convinced the priest of the Real Presence,"
rose straight up like a Sunday hat, with a black-
and-white striped ribbon woven through
the intricate herringbone straw-colored brick.
Or a herd of zebras, all eyes and legs and hide.
Inside the chapel, on the long south wall, angels guided
The Blessed to Paradise (the fresco was especially lurid,
as if light couldn't be anything but blinding) and beyond them
was the same hillside we had seen outside,
winding up to that very spot,
which as I remember it
was covered with poppies.

Red, red everywhere: the poppies, the altar cloth, the red stripe
of paint that marks the collar of the brown dog who darts
at Dante's feet in the fresco as he watches the pilgrimage—
a pearl necklace of souls spiraling to heaven.
The front of the cathedral, the side facing the piazza,
was bandaged with drop cloths and struts of scaffolding.
The repairs must be finished now, or begun again.
What were we doing there, in Orvieto, looking
and looking until we were dizzy? Who, even
then, was *we*, and who was *I*, that *I* that was heading
toward you, now that once again
one instant of your gray gaze has smote
the barking dog, the scudding rain,
the piazza, turning them ghostly as if they never were?
Striped cool fell on my bare arms and legs
in a grotto of shade beside the cathedral.
The ice cream tasted faintly of grass
and was cold on my tongue as last night

before the rain started, holding a cold glass of green wine
labeled Orvieto, I looked at a row of books and couldn't
    remember
which page held the scene I was looking for—
the black-and-white shadow of the balustrade in an old house,
the dog begging scraps from the table
and two people on the landing who pulled away
from each other a moment too soon, that flick of the curtain
a teardrop, eyelet along the sill
caught but fluttering—

the way the dove in the fountain in Ravenna, where I went
the next week (each inch of her a separate glittering stone)
held her wings open in the water in the basin
where the hairlines of mortar were studded
with viridian moss, a few tiny angel wings unfolding
now that the ice is broken—the dog out for a walk
pausing to drink, shaking his fur as he lifts his head
each drop mercurial, a convex mirror, an open eye
silver against the fountain's upturned dark blue stone cup.

HERMES, 1981

Bird bones barely hardened, a river
of blue vein, hyacinth blue, you
reached for the lintel—if desire
were meat I would hold that moment
      forever in my mouth.

POEM

Shell or skull, ship hull, the sail star-flecked, trefoil,
your hand a lure, coaxing my mouth, sloughing
catching and quick holding, black moon salt and the rowing
       to the reed-slick bank, hard—

there again, and again, oar dipping, finding the channel,
then battering, Odysseus in the grey dawn light returning
fast in the phosphorescent water, churning
       the froth and pine-sweet smell of tar.

LATE POEM

"... a matter of changing a slide in a magic lantern."

I wish we were Indians and ate foie gras
and drove a gas-guzzler
and never wore seat belts

I'd have a baby, yours, *cette fois,*
and I'd smoke Parliaments
and we'd drink our way through the winter

in spring the baby would laugh at the moon
who is her father and her mother who is his pool
and we'd walk backwards and forwards

in lizard-skin cowboy boots
and read *Gilgamesh* and *Tintin* aloud
I'd wear only leather or feathers

plucked from endangered birds and silk
from exploited silkworms
we'd read *The Economist*

it would be before and after the internet
I'd send you letters by carrier pigeons
who would only fly from one window

to another in our drafty, gigantic house
with twenty-three uninsulated windows
and the dog would be always be

off his leash and always
find his way home as we will one day
and we'd feed small children

peanut butter and coffee in their milk
and I'd keep my hand glued under your belt
even while driving and cooking

and no one would have our number
except I would have yours where I've kept it
carved on the sole of my stiletto

which I would always wear when we walked
in the frozen and dusty wood
and we would keep warm by bickering

and falling into bed perpetually and
entirely unsafely as all the best things are
—your skin and my breath on it.

OLD-FASHIONED POEM

The truth is I always think of you.
The garden is beautiful as a folktale—
speedwell, oxalis, and foxglove,
white moths above the foamflower.
What would it be like I wonder
    if want were set as song,
to sit with you in the evening, my life's love,
as cats eye bees in the bee balm
and the shade grows long?

FIRST FLY

"She had kept only a few—mainly botanical and entomological—pages of her diary."

The first fly of summer buzzing at the window—
palpable, its anxiety to *get out*
furious as if the letters were a door:
get's harsh strokes, a stirrup, stop, and bar, then the round vowels,

the fly bashing its head to get through *out*'s omphalos
where the dew-silvered leaves of the cherry tree
outside the window rim the arched edge
of the universe which is everywhere but

here, on the ledge, where the radiator vent
stamped with openwork fleur-de-lis
is a trapdoor to—nowhere. It's not the *o*
after all but the *u* (*you?*) of *out,* that's (possibly) the problem.
    The fly, enormous

in its hatred of being bound,
takes one sticky leg, an eyelash, and vaults over the horseshoe,
lucky for him, and uses *t*'s bar to launch himself out on glassine
    wings:
pure blue, endless. The rain

has stopped. The sun, hot as a magnifying glass,
burns holes in the cherry leaves, each one an impossibly
remote star guiding the way to a planet, any planet, impossibly
    far—
until the latch of the world slams shut on its spy hole.

Gone, the fly, all frenzy, my beating heart.

METAPHYSICAL POEM

When before sleep I close my eyes,
I see instead of nebulae
your face focused by your grave gaze—
a numismatist's gem—a pair
doubled, so we are eye-to-eye,
hazel wood rimmed by sea and sky
by now ten times a thousand days;
and when dull coins do close my lids,
it will be your sly eye I bid
to come to marry mine amazed.

MIDNIGHT IN JULY

"A pretty plaything stranded among the forget-me-nots . . ."

Then, in an instant, there we were again—

> " *'But* this, *this is certain,' exclaimed Ada, 'this is pure fact—this moss,*
> *your hand, the ladybird on my leg,*
> *this cannot be taken away, can it?' (it will, it was).*

the air remembered us, and the moon
knew us too, her face our fingerprint—

> 'This *has all come together* here, *no matter how the paths*
> *twisted and fooled each other, and got fouled up*
> *they inevitably met here!'*

the blur of white clover a city seen
from a cloud, and you laughed, your

hand on my hip marking it as it's been
marked all this time, the bird in my throat

knit of mist and clover skittering,
keening, finding the word in that flower

> *'We must now find our bicycles,' said Van, 'we are lost*
> *in another part of the forest.'*

that has belonged only to you, the moon
drinking the night as if it were water—

> *'Oh let's not return yet,' she cried, 'oh wait!'* "

FOURTH DREAMSCAPE
(ALEXANDRINE: ROXANE AND STATIERA)

"(I suggest omitting this little chapter altogether. Ada's note.)"

In the dream your wife called to tell me you were dead.
She said, this is 'X,' I have some news. We hadn't
spoken before but there was little, I could tell,
she didn't know. I said I was sorry. She knew
I wasn't sorry I loved you. I love you still.
'Z' was driving. Why? I asked, knowing that you were
afraid of bridges. You have no wife. The dream said:
You have no life. There was a boat, a skiff—the line
bloodied my hand. 'X' waited for me, it went on,
my screaming. We decided to meet quite soon, once
we'd both "calmed down." She—'X'—was calm. It was kind—of
her, I thought, to include herself in my dreaming.

FUGUE: PILGRIM VALLEY

Again I find myself in tears—find myself,
that lost one—asleep at noon beneath
the gazebo's furrowed brow. Yesterday
I took the ferry and drove south inside
summer's buzzing gong: Clotho, a spider
letting her silk pulley down along each
capillary lane, stippled with tiger lilies,
their garnet throats rimmed with kohl above wild
carrot ruffs, a bleached galaxy—Queen Anne's
openwork plied to make heads turn. The past's
clear colors make the future dim, Lethe's
swale laced with willow twigs. Nothing happened
without you. I want you to see what I see—
I'm talking with your fingers caught in my mouth.

HEARING VOICES

" 'I remember the cards,' she said, 'and the light and the noise of the rain.' "

A house exactly like yours, dare-devil,
straddling a stream, the river god pushing
a joke, this once, too far, wind tearing humpback
clouds to shreds. Enraged, your Morse code slurs: "Sunday,
we'll have to move for water calm enough
to fish," then, gnomon, leaping trout: "We're headed—
hah—for the Two-Hearted River—I want you
here *right now*, but that's just me." *Tu me manques,
mon frère.* The house gleams, a cardboard dacha—
heat lightning makes the diamond windows wink.
Upstream, Bach jitterbugs. *"She likes what all
our belles like . . . balls, orchids, and the Cherry Orchard—"*
Elms plow the ground. After the storm, vapor
rises from the cropped field like dry ice.

FROM *THE BOOK OF KNOWLEDGE*

(*THE CHILDREN'S ENCYCLOPEDIA*/ THE GROLIER SOCIETY, VOL. 115, 1936)

" 'For the snake of a rhyme,' cried Ada."

1. What makes a fairy ring?
    Fairy rings are made of a kind of fungus.

2. Why does damp air make us ill?
    *Damp air is often cold air, and the cold has usually been blamed for
    making us ill, though many facts prove that it is not blameworthy at all.*

3. Why does a dog go round and round before it lies down?
    The answer to this question lies in another question. What is a dog?

4. Can our brains ever fill up?
    The poet Browning says "there is no end to learning."

5. Why does a tuning fork sound louder when it touches
    wood?
    *The sound from a tuning fork, like the light from a candle, flows out
    in all directions.*

6. Why are some things poisonous?
    *We could only answer this question completely and fully if we knew
    all there is to know about life.*

7. Why can we hear better when we shut our eyes?
    This question is partly true and partly not true.

8. Can an animal think?
    There is no doubt an animal can think, and that it can remember.

9. Do animals feel pain as we do?
   That is not a question that can be answered directly.

10. Why do we not growl like animals when we are hungry?
    A hungry man is an angry man.

11. Why have leaves different shapes?
    The great idea which we learn to apply to every fact about living creatures is that these facts usually have uses.

12. Why do the leaves of the aspen always shake?
    The shaking of the leaves has the same effect as if the trees were fanning themselves.

13. Why does oil make a wheel go round more easily?
    It all depends on where the oil is put.

14. Why do we see the stars only at night?
    The stars are shining all the time, sending light to earth, but more than this is needed for us to see.

15. Is an atom alive?
    It is almost a living thing.

16. Can country people see "writ small" better than townspeople?
    If country folk use their eyes mainly at distances, their vision will be keenest at distances.

17. Why does a lump rise in my throat when I cry?
    It is the place of speech which is the most marvelous thing.

EARLY AUGUST: FLYCATCHER ROAD

" 'But now I think I should have taken the risk of speaking, of stammering.' "

By now what we want equals what we owe.
Where will we live in heaven if there is no heaven?
On the island called "You're Not Here"—hold-all,
my head doesn't have room for all it's asked
to hold. "I think we're slipping into time
apart. I think you don't know enough about
'S'—she's her mother's daughter, brilliantly
astute, aware of the suspicions in
the house." Rainbow cat's cradle, tethered
to a bough—when we had whole cloth we bound
ourselves like Hamlet's nattering ghost in rags.
Poor story that bites its sorry tail; your coat
of tar, our Götterdämmerung of air—
stone-winged, it breathes and fossils what we touch.

AT COW HOLLOW

The bay is watered silk, then convex, a mirror
holding a clutch of sleepers, brown-eyed pansies,
their irises topaz, planetary.
I wonder if you think of me. Rain at dawn;
at dusk, the water crepe de chine, the sky
reversed: washed minarets, the urchins' pinchbeck
turbans strewn to dry. In New York, our local
seeress, Madame Amphitrite, hangs
out her shingle: *By Appointment Only,*
Two to Four. Left on my own five minutes,
I don't know whether to weep or sleep.
The life I have without you goes on without me—
far out, a catboat locked in rainbow haze.
Moths shatter the sun with their burnt wings.

MEMENTO MORI

The first time I left you,
  the first
     time—I mean to say—
         I left when you did,
    I went oystering every day
  on the Cow's Neck flats—
         low tide a mirror
             broken to a million bits
      the gulls screaming
        hungry hungry
       guilty guilty
         quit quit
     and because I didn't have a knife
  I steamed them open, the salt vapor
      like lace, and they opened lavender,
         silver,
    frilled—
        each one a moth—
  les étoiles, rank,
      shivering.

THE DAMSELFLY (SECOND FLY)

"Oh who will render in our tongue
the tender things he loved and sung?"

I knew a green damsel cut to the quick.
I don't know why she was cut to the quick—
what made her tick?

I knew a bright damsel who danced on a pin.
She danced to a tune day out and day in.
I don't know why it cut her to the quick.
What made her tick?

I knew a quick damsel cut to the marrow,
who girt her wings eluding a sparrow—
a sparrow trilling who sang in her marrow.
I don't know why she felt cut to the quick.
What made her tick?

I knew a chaste damsel who could sing—
a ruby-throat who folded her wings.
She girt her wings to elude the sparrow,
wanton and quick, who sang to her marrow.
I don't know why the bird cut to the quick.
What made her tick?

I knew a damsel, hungry and slight,
who stepped from the water in a cap of light—
she slipped from the shallows shaking her wings,
eluding the sparrow whose burdensome song
pleaded, *too-wit,* and pulsed in her marrow.

What does it mean to be cut to the quick?
What made her tick?

I knew a bronze damsel who spun light,
shielding the cloud that shadowed her flight,
and kept her, alit, from eluding the sparrow
whose song, piquant, ran through her marrow
—but that shadow's the sparrow, a conjuring trick,
quicksilver frayed by time's cross-stitch—
quicker and tighter it cut to the quick.
What made her tick?

I once knew a damsel who wanted to fly.
Slight narrow rudder, sapphire nymph
who waited for wings, whose *mph*
propelled her, whirring, to light on the mallow.
But how did she think she'd elude the sparrow,
whose repeating song, too incessantly high
strummed and sung in her marrow?
I don't know why she was so very quick.
What made her tick?

I knew a dry damsel, ragged and shy,
who tore at her wings, or maybe was shorn,
who lit on a stalk to elude the sparrow
whose song, stinging, clung to her marrow
—the sparrow, his shade stitched to a shadow

beside whom, pure nerve, she hovered
stalking the air as if her beloved.
Air she had, and that endless awful song.
I don't know why she was cut to the quick.
What made her tick?

AT SUNFLOWER FARM

"(Ada: 'They are now practically extinct at Ardis.')"

Instead of Cyclops' eye, the phoenix, infra-
red: Sebastian's gold ring in his mouth,
his herded arrows silver birds, their wings
tipped with poisoned wood. When Solzhenitsyn
moved to Pomfret his neighbors posted signs:
NO DIRECTIONS TO THE SOLZHENITSYNS.
Dead, since we've spoken. Crab-claw of ice, when
Cúchulain slew the waves he knew he'd lost.
Each wrong I do rescores my palm's triplet
life line. Entrails, outmoded—my played-out
pride, like pot or protest; the Anglo-Saxon
that we learned lockstep taught us fate not choice.
Love, look: the bronze sunflower whose seed face
scatters without the seed tearing apart.

WHITE PANSIES, SEPTEMBER

White storm of winter pansies
and the calico cat on the counter
who puts her paw into the milk jug
swiftly, secretly—as I think of you
—the sweet taste on her paw raised
to her mouth again, and again.

COLUMBUS DAY POEM

If we love what vanishes then what stays?
In the dream I was a child running in a rice paddy
my footprint a damp butterfly wing—a Morpho,
its shot-silk sky blue rimmed with black. "Don't
they know," said Lowell, crossing Harvard Yard,
"that all my poems are about heartbreak?"
Your lashes inches from the phone's tin ear:
"The irony that is my life, I'm home
to make dinner for a Dutch exchange student;
what I need is organization—other
people have affairs." Lamprey, electric
eel, stingray—electrocardiogram,
blueprint maps the Morpho's gas-lit loop-de-loop.
How do we love what we've lost—or not?

OBLIQUE STRATEGIES

"She also knows my revised monologue of his mad king."

I   IS SOMETHING MISSING?

But what of the rest? The King of Hearts, the Queen
of Diamonds—just discarded? Jack of Clubs
and King of Spades, and all their raggle-taggle
retinue? Time and space demand their due
—not just Murder-Mad John and Memory Queen,
his blood muse: for in the green-gold world's
bright ring, sleek traveler between fresh water
and brisk air, you wed in real time and for love.
And those babes, dressed in your old cobweb clothes
—mercury, King's Lynn silk, fey dappled moon—
not changelings, those, but your dear dread own,
paramorph whose name seesaws. By now
the planet's face, seen from that star, has changed
its phase: your raven hair is stippled grey.

II   IS IT FINISHED?

These new cards contain oblique strategies—
silo, elm, hawk, balloon-with-basket—stunned
sky's spider sac—but however the cards
are laid they match, a landscape made of fits
and starts, where what has happened once is chance.
We might have guessed. But asked if the scorched world

is flat, the mantel's lineup draws a blank.
Blown chaff aloft above the mapmaker's
punning palindrome, your wavering sky-
blue script—"my hand on my heart, I swear"—
reads: "(a) ware my heart is on your hands,"
and then, pale moth of winged hot air, alights
in your cupped fingers. The tap's a tear jet.
Hot water, dear one, for your scald hand.

III   WHAT IS REALITY?

Bangles, mascara wand, a boutonniere,
cornflower blue in your seersucker lapel—
if I had told you thirty years ago
we'd make this drive, wouldn't you have been
surprised? Why, Ada, no. Why would I be?
I told you I would love you forever,
and I do. Now I need two hands to drive
beneath Neue Dublin's frozen zodiac.
These Russian winters remind me of my
childhood, smoking roofs, icicle scimitars,
Dim Jack playing chicken until the goosegirl melts—
so let's drive back before it gets too dark.
(The King of Spades demoted to a murmur;
your palindrome inside his mortal shade.)

IV   WHAT WOULDN'T YOU DO?

Why, it's a journey to the land that time
forgot-me-not. When the Jack of Clubs
dressed you in ambergris and myrrh, his skin
was alabaster. I've never not loved
that you loved me: as always, never better
than she ought to be, "love ADA" morphs to "love
ADD"—Miss Print of the soul's type, "let's pretend."
Romance, whose sole recourse is roundabout,
I find myself in missing you—the matrix,
oblique as Jupiter's reflected gaze
makes each fourteen a prism'd twenty-eight.
As Juno, Queen of Heaven, not of cards,
looks on, in lieu—but not instead—of love.
But now to get on with our piebald story.

IRISH POEM

I looked for want
and want I found
where'er I went
over blent ground
my heart I stilled
my ear I bent
but not a word
or sound I heard.

I looked for want
dumb heart in two
no sound or word
but what I found
was what it meant—
where'er I went
I could not find
my own blind bird.

I looked for want
where'er I went
with my heart rent
and what I found
was bone split too—
a raven's nest
my eye did find
and a bird blind.

My heart in two
was my own heart
the coal black bird
was my own ear

that heard no sound
nor would come near
that song too dear
for me to hear.

I looked for want
and want I found
my name is want
no song, no sound
the whitened ground
is where I went
I took my heart
where the road bent.

Now hare, my heart
I say to you
what is the sound
that these bones meant
to play upon
the trees' bent boughs?
In accident
the song did start—

where the road bent
my heart did part.
I looked for want
and want I found—
I wanted want
for I was meant
to hear the sound
of what I heard
since love did start.

CODA

These fitful poems are our daft child—
first wonder, faith's blue eye, the green-blue planet's almost haze
    that lifts, clouds' gauze and lingering storm shade

           then fists beating, half merman,
  half wraith, a leaping herring
wrapped in newsprint's thrice-printed ink—
        that plaided quarto is your gift, and mine.
    The icon, that cast die, and not ever once being warm
           so looking for warmth, that tartan

             a green copse, re-crossed with Chinese red,
        its runnels watered blood—the poet dipped
        his pen in water twice

  so the fawn, its fur spattered with blurred stars
         won't turn and bolt
but stay fast, indefinitely—
    gaze fixed by the headlight's hazel.

Pine tree in snow, the bled herringbone's woven spire
  its star reading the wood's tea leaves,

what makes the hunter dear and the deer the hunter?
    Love must be put
  into action—this is the action.

NOTES

Throughout the text, quotes from *Ada, or Ardor: A Family Chronicle*, by Vladimir Nabokov (McGraw-Hill, 1969) are represented by italics within quotation marks.

p. v—"To sing about someone you love is one thing, but, oh,
the blood's hidden guilty river-god is something else."
—Rainer Maria Rilke, *Duino Elegies*, the
Sonnets to Orpheus ("The Third Elegy")
translated by A. Poulin, Jr. (Houghton Mifflin, 1977)

"No one escapes love or death."
—Syrus, *Maxims*

"Third Dreamscape"—The scene on the stairway in this section's final stanza appears in a novel by William Maxwell, *The Château* (Alfred A. Knopf, 1961).

"Fourth Dreamscape"—Roxane (literally, "luminous beauty" or "little star") was the first wife of Alexander the Great. She killed Alexander's second wife, Statiera, after his death.

"Oblique Strategies" is a card game devised by the musician Brian Eno and the artist Peter Schmidt in 1975. A question is written on each card; the player draws a card at random when in life or work he finds himself at an impasse. In Section II, The Endless Landscape or "myriorama" (meaning "many views") was a popular nineteenth-century card game: the painted scenes on the cards can be lined up in any sequence to create a harmonious vista.

ACKNOWLEDGMENTS

Grateful acknowledgment is made to *The Paris Review*, *The Yale Review*, *The American Scholar*, and *Epiphany*, where some of these poems appeared in slightly different form.

"Poem for a Printing Press" was first printed as a letterpress broadside by Nicholas McBurney for the Berkeley College Press at Yale College, in an edition of fifty copies, numbered and signed by the author.

For their help in the preparation of this manuscript, the author would like to thank Deborah Garrison, Caroline Zancan, Langdon Hammer, and Martin Edmunds—*Возьми ж на радость дикий мой подаро*— and The MacDowell Colony, for two residencies over two winters.

A NOTE ON THE TYPE

The text of this book was set in Centaur, the only typeface designed by Bruce Rogers (1870–1957), the well-known American book designer. A celebrated penman, Rogers based his design on the roman face cut by Nicolas Jenson in 1470 for his Eusebius. Jenson's roman surpassed all of its forerunners and even today, in modern recuttings, remains one of the most popular and attractive of all typefaces.

The italic used to accompany Centaur is Arrighi, designed by another American, Frederic Warde, and based on the chancery face used by Lodovico degli Arrighi in 1524.

COMPOSED BY

North Market Street Graphics, Lancaster, Pennsylvania

PRINTED AND BOUND BY

Thomson-Shore, Dexter, Michigan

DESIGNED BY

Iris Weinstein